Mysteries of Voice

Mysteries of Voice
...robust and timely revelation

Mysteries of Voice
...robust and timely revelation

Omoniyi A. Akinnuwa

Mysteries of Voice -
...robust and timely revelation

Copyright ©2008 by Omoniyi A. Akinnuwa

Published by: Divine Voice Impact
Unit 4, Dartmouth industrial Centre,
Kylemore Road, Dublin 10, Republic of Ireland

All Scripture, unless otherwise stated, are taken from the New King James
Version of the Bible. Copyright 1979, 1980, 1982, 1990, Thomas Nelson Inc.

ISBN: 978-0-9559368-0-7
Cover design + layout by: vixionart.com
Printed in Ireland by vixions

Endorsements

I recommend this book for serious, close to the heart reading by everyone- Christians and non-Christians alike. You cannot read it and still remain the same. Your life pattern will be positively affected. Read it for your benefit. Read it to get liberated from the negative voices of your detractors. Read it to live above the realm of the ungodly. Read it to insulate yourself against the evil imaginations of the mind. You can become your own deliverer and that of your generation in Christ.

Pastor (Prof.) S.O Ewuola.

God through his prophetic voice will through this book change your mindset and your language so that you can begin to speak as "god"-"commanding those things that are not as though they were" and employing the creative force of prophetic words to change the atmosphere, do the impossible and keep the devil and his cohort forever at bay in your generation. This book is loaded with uncommon concepts, insights, ideas and testimonies to help you operate at a higher dimension in God. I hereby recommend it to every serious minded Christians.

Pastor Sunday J.Adu
Maryland, U.S.A

Evangelist Niyi shares a powerful message that every Christian need to hear. The level of the teaching is absolutely incredible. You are hearing from somebody who knows what he is talking about. The depth of his teaching, its interdenominational flavour with anointed power is unbeatable. I sincerely recommend this anointed book for you.

Pastor John O. Fasan
Senior Pastor GFM Ireland.

This is a timely revelation by God to his servant Evangelist Omoniyi Akinnuwa. It is a must read to all who desire to be a voice not an echo, original not a photocopy in this our generation like John the Baptist, who was the voice that cried in the wilderness.

Evangelist Victor O. Akilla
G. O Victory of the Cross Bible Church.

ℱoreword

A voice is an identity, a revealer of the present state of mind as well as the minds plan for the future. It can be a powerful tool of offensive as well a defensive nature. By it one can rise, by it another can fall. It can be a potent determinant of fate and future.

This book, mysteries of voice reveals the mind of the author and his attitude to voice." It is a power packed book generously supplied with rich real life experiences. It reveals the word of God as supreme and unquestionable. Believe it for your living. Accept it for your victory. Use it for your success.

Pastor (Prof.) S.O Ewuola
Deputy G.O, Gospel Faith Mission Int.

Mysteries of Voice

Acknowledgements

This book is an absolute inspiration of the Holy Spirit. It became real to me how the Bible was written by inspiration. I appreciate the exposure to the knowledge and ministerial experience I have placed in this work, through his divine assistance. Holy Spirit you are sweet.

To Pastor & Mrs Emmanuel Akinnuwa, my friend and model in faith Evangelist Victor Akilla, Evangelist Dr. E.O Falade for the word of Knowledge about this project. I cherish your lives and the part it plays in mine.

To Professor S.O Ewuola, Pastor Sunday Adu, Pastor & Mrs John Fasan, Bro Clem and Bro Femi & Ruth Hezekiah. Thank you for all the supports you gave me.

To our children, and my dear wife who consistently motivate, encourage and pray for the actualization of my academic and ministerial commitments. My achievements are yours, also.

Dedication

To God the creator of heaven and earth who through the
Holy sprit motivated me to write this book.
To my father, Pastor Andrew Akinnuwa and my mother
Deaconess Felicia Taiwo Akinnuwa. A prayerful parent like
you is rare. The legacy of faith you deliver to us is priceless.
We love you always.
To my mother in-law, Deaconess Oluwatoyin Shanu you
are a true mother.
To all, who desire to fulfil their assignment on earth and are
ready to create their world by their voice.

Mysteries of Voice

Contents

Introduction

Lack of access to the mysteries of voice can make life miserable. Voice is an important integral part of every human being and some mammalian creatures. Understanding the anatomy and physiology of voice in relation to tongue is a powerful mechanism in human system of communication.

The dictionary defines that voice is produced in the larynx and uttered through the mouth, as a speech or song. Voice (or vocalization) is the sound produced by humans and other vertebrates using the lungs and the vocal folds in the larynx, or voice box. Voice is not always produced as speech. However, Infants babble and coo; animals bark, moo, whinny, growl, and meow; and adult humans laugh.

Voice is an opinion or the right to express an opinion. Communication becomes impossible at some level without a voice; man can do much with voice and little without it. Henry Wadsworth Longfellow quipped "the human voice is the organ of the soul".

There is nothing more common among men, no human activity more universal, yet more mysterious and misunderstood, than voice.

Some studies have even validated the effectiveness of voice on physiological and behavioural responses of human beings and stress the effect on human development and socialization.

The president of the United States has a voice, the prime minister of Israel has it, and the Pope has it, Christian, Muslim, Hindus, Pagans, children, adult, Satan and God have it. Even terrorists have a voice. No matter how diverse the culture, religions and beliefs of the world may be, voice is one common way humans embrace to express their opinion.

God himself changed the order of the world in which darkness was prevalent. By His voice darkness gave way for light without contest. It has been so from the beginning and will continue to be till the world will cease. The first man fell from grace at a yield to the voice of the Serpent this therefore suggests, that serpent can speak in the earliest plan of creation.

Is voice really powerful, do my uses, reactions or responses to voice have any impact on my life? The mysteries which surround the power of voice that is universally undermined and misappropriated is what inspired me with the help of the Holy Spirit to write this book.

Let us begin by taking a journey through the land of doubt, shedding the scepticism and activating the awesome power of voice every human being possess: the power that influenced the earth from heaven, which caused what was not to be, produced light and separated day and night. The voice of God marked the first ground braking record of separation method which is now a routine in the scientific world.

Chapter

Mysteries of voice unfold

Voice is one of the major characteristic features of many living organisms. It is such a powerful weapon backed up with an invisible awesome power. It is a universal asset that has much importance as time. With voice you can identify, on many occasions who is speaking or who is in charge. Voice is such a powerful weapon in the spiritual and material world. It can construct or deconstruct, encourage or discourage, heal or make sick.

A merry heart does good, like medicine, But a broken spirit dries the bones (Prove 17:22).

Some voices can dry the bones of excitement, ability and inspiration. It can sentence to life or death, lift up or pull down, can lead to oppression, enslave or emancipate, build hope or abort hope. Voice can impact the past, present and future. Voice can bring about the aforementioned when represented in oral or written form.

Voice is so powerful and vital in all human operations; in government, administration, church, family, educational institutions, politics, business, relationship the list is endless.

In any community voice is such a vital weapon in the response and the command of government attention to the need of various faction and sector that is represented either as majority or minority group. It is a means to convey the needs, interests, plights and concerns of people. When the voice of a minority can not be heard in a constituency, they are bound to suffer set backs. Even in the program of God, the same principle applies; God responds to the cry or voice of his children with passion and urgency.

I said earlier that voice is an expression of opinion or intentions. Let me show you other mysterious truths you must know on the subject of voice.

You need to realize that tapes, letters, navigator and written documents are a voice. Before you secure a contract you make a proposal that is, your voice is presented in written words with or without your conspicuous presence and your intention is known. Similarly, the voice of the world's Prime terrorist could be heard in his hiding place on tape (voice over tape). Curriculum vitae or resume is a voice it clearly states to a potential employer what you can do and why you should be considered for that position. Your business card is your voice; it describes your operations. Written verdict by a judge is a voice.

Your cheque book is your voice authorizing a particular payment thus it's a criminal offence to forge it. Letter from bank granting or declining an application is a voice of a person deciding the issue. Yes is a voice and No is a voice. I have had experiences with voice saying, we regret you are not successful at this time or am' sorry I can't help you this time but I have refused to give in to them and because I voiced back, these voices have been reversed in my favour on many occasions.

Your bill is a voice advising you how much you have incurred on your Phone, gas, electricity and so on. Such a voice should not be buried. If you throw it away or keep it without appropriate response, it will come again even with a louder voice that is, huge bills. A search or arrest warrant is a voice from the Police. People's vote is their voice, signs on the road are a voice and it makes life easy for motorist when properly designed. To sign in or out at work is a voice saying, 'you resume work or finish at a given time'.

Finally, the Bible is the voice of God believe it or not. He honours his word (voice) more than his name. At this point, you can greatly appreciate and admit that voice is powerful and mysterious it is a universal asset. In fact, voice is a weapon. "There is no index of character as sure as the voice" (Benjamin Disraeli).

Voice, has the following elements or properties; Identification, Information, Mission, Direction and Instruction.

PROPERTIES OF VOICE

Identification

Deuteronomy 5: 24 (NKJV)

*And you said: 'surely the LORD our **God** has shown us His glory and His greatness, and we have heard His **voice** from the midst of the fire. We have seen this day that **God** speaks with man; yet he still lives.*

Here, the voice from the midst of fire identified a supreme personality. They knew it was a voice they were unfamiliar with. Not of Moses or anybody else. Most parents like me can identify who among their children is saying hello. Genders can be easily identified sometimes by voice as well friends from enemy, Pastors can easily recognize their members with voice in fact, God recognized his sheep. He can juxtapose sinners and saint's voice at the same time. Thus, the use of voice for identification cannot be underestimated or overemphasised.

With voice, it could be identified who is talking or in charge. His personality was not mistaken for somebody else. Jesus said, *my **sheep** hear my voice, and I **know** them, and they follow **Me**. (John 10:27).* Here again, Jesus established the identity of his followers by demonstrating the knowledge of their voices.

Information

Genesis 18:17 And the LORD said, "Shall I hide from Abraham what I am doing,

Voice is an important access point to information. An uninformed individual is a deformed person. In times past and in the present, voice has been so instrumental in information dissemination to generations, individuals and heroes of faith. Yielding to this voice is a matter of choice. What information does is to provide opportunity for a change and your response to it determines your choice for either change or chains. Information could be definite, precise or non definite. God gave a promise to Abraham, he had an idea he's in the program of God, yet the time of its materialization was not actually divulged. There has been information leading to victory and conquest, Abraham's future was detailed to him by the voice of God. Hence, it becomes so vital to discover the secret of wealth and greatness with voice.

Many are beating about the bush today because there has not been a voice to lead them; they have laboured in vain and wasted their potential resources. My prayer is that the Lord will send a voice to you to redirect your path from destruction and order your steps into a total recovery for perfect restoration.

There is an informational voice you need to guide you, you are not there in reality, but you capture what is going to happen there. With a voice of instruction, a journey of days could be completed in four days. It prevents abuse of purpose. Many are confused and in dilemma today of what to do, where to go and how to do it because there is no voice to inform. It is time for you to embark on and do great things and get good results when you understand this mystery.

Direction

This is a union brother to information; I'll say voice of direction has the attribute or sense of specificity. It optimizes time and maximizes resources. It is indispensable spiritual software necessary to experience skyrocketed promotion. This is the secret of celebrities. They know where they are going, what they are doing and pursue it defiantly while dealing ruthlessly with any obstacle. It is a driver of the optimists and a navigator for many who have excelled in life and ministry.

Voice of direction grants speed to business, ministry, family and career. It prevents the syndrome of majoring on the minor. It averts squandering and misappropriation of resources. It is a key to supernatural abundance and escape from likely disappointments. If you go to the wrong person for help in time of dare need lacking a voice of direction, you will come back with genuine excuses leaving you depressed.

ABUNDANCE IN TIME OF SCARCITY

1 kings 17:9-10 (NKJV)
"Go at once to Zarephath of Sidon and stay there. I have commanded a widow in that place to supply you with food."
So he went to Zarephath. When he came to the town gate, a widow was there gathering sticks. He called to her and asked, "Would you bring me a little water in a jar so I may have a drink?"

Elijah the prophet escaped starvation when the voice directed him to the widow of Zarephat not somewhere else or another widow elsewhere who might have the meals he needed for survival but not ready to give .What a specific direction.

Those who have enjoyed this voice of direction in their journey of life are always on top and people will say; they are lucky. In the name of Jesus, you're the next on line.

Mission

Mark 11; 12-14, 20-21(NKJV)

Now the next day, when they had come out from Bethany, He was hungry. And seeing from afar a fig tree having leaves, He went to see if perhaps He would find something on it. When He came to it, He found nothing but leaves, for it was not the season for figs. In response Jesus said to it "Let no one eat fruit from you ever again." And His disciples heard it Now in the morning, as they passed by, they saw the fig tree dried up from the roots. And Peter, remembering, said to Him, "Rabbi, look! The fig tree which you cursed has withered away." **(Effect of voice in less than 24 hours)**

The account of the scripture above shows that voice function to achieve specific goal or assignment. Whenever it is uttered the higher and lower classes of creature respond to this stimulus. The fig tree heard and obeyed the voice of Jesus, it became fruitless at the voice of Jesus and it dried completely. This demonstrates the incredible power of voice.

Many lives have been withered by voices of men but I have come to say to you there is hope. The tree of your life will become fresh again

Here is an outcome of a research which demonstrates the physiological effects of voice, how voice can mar or make lives. There were two flower plants subjected to the same condition of growth, both were watered, pruned and equally cared for but there was something different about them; to one of these flowers every blessed morning, something good will be pronounced on it like what a beautiful flower, so lovely, attractive, bright, and while the other flower was treated on the opposite in regard to these.

This continued over a reasonable period of time and when the time came to assess them, the one with pleasant vocal treatment looked more healthy and attractive than the other on the negative end.

Here comes the great vocal impact even though they are both flowers of the same species what made the difference between them was the voice.

I read the story of a young man called Ben Carson (a renowned Neuron-surgeon today). When he was in high school, he was the class dummy; but his mother kept saying to him, **"Ben, if anybody can do anything, you can do better"**.

Today he is recognized as the man who successfully separated Siamese twins joined skull to skull. That operation took them twenty-two hours, with a team of seventy surgeons. Ben Carson was the head of the team he is making rounds around the world. It will also interest you to know that Ben is a black American- so, black is not synonymous with deficiency. See the influence of voice in the mouth of a positive mother who understands the power in voice.

Listen, this condition cannot last forever if you can employ the weaponry of voice constructively; your son, daughter, wife and husband can change. Voice can change that condition to a desirable position. Understand this, that every voice has a mission so, do not take or handle it with levity.

A real life story; I ministered to a woman about a year ago; she lend an intimate friend of hers a huge sum of money for a particular business which eventually hit the rock. Due to her insistence on the repayment of which she had no means, she employed the service of an Islamic prophet from her native country; that through voice attacked her like Balaam was hired.

At a particular time she knew her friend was planning to visit her native country, the voice struck to make her vulnerable. Such that if she travelled, she will never have any opportunity to come back to the country she resides and the debt will be cancelled. After this, she mysteriously found herself in a complex immigration mess beyond human explanation.

This plan was revealed during prayer when the voice of the perpetrator spoke through her and the cause of her plight was uncovered, to the glory of God today, that plan was reversed and she's happily living in Ireland.

Numbers 22: 3-6 (NKJV)

The exodus of the Israelite witnessed a vocal attack in order to control their expansion and enlargement; the Midianites were threatened by their settlement next to them and went to employ the service of a prophet's voice to do what? To curse the people of God so that they would be vulnerable to his attack on the ground that the people of God were too mighty for him and that they might drive them out of their land. It therefore became so clear here, the mission of a voice.

In the name of Jesus, every voice assigned to evacuate you from your land of rest or to curse you, will bless you in return.

I don't care who and how your life has been injured, battered or withered through voice, you will experience a dramatic restoration. Voices, such as described above have architected the downfall of many businesses, calamities of many children, tragedy of many homes and retardation of progress. I don't know which voice is on a mission in your life, family or ministry as far as the mission is deadly and destructive, it will not bear fruit in the name of Jesus.

As you are reading through this book, every voice affecting your past, your family, and career, hurting your present and hunting your future will be silenced by the supreme voice in the name of Jesus. You will be free from any negative voice controlling your life and family in Jesus name.

<u>PRAY ALONG</u>

- I activate in the name of Jesus voice of direction in my life
- I activate in the name of Jesus voice of instruction in my life
- I activate in the name of Jesus voice of information in my life
- I deactivate every voice of confusion in my life in the name of Jesus.
- I command to wither and dry the trees and fruits of evil voice in my live.

Chapter

2

Classification of Voice

Voice of prophets

Hosea 12:13(NKJV).By *a prophet the LORD brought Israel out of Egypt, and by a prophet he was preserved.*

Who is a prophet? A prophet stands to convey celestial information, instruction and directions to a nation, individual, family even business. No prophet known so far is biologically dumb because their voice is their power .They have the tendency to migrate destiny from darkness to light, from obscurity to limelight by the unquestionable vocal attribute assigned of their office.

No man must live in isolation you need a prophet in your life. This could be your pastor, your evangelist, priest, minister that have spiritual update and sensitivity, to navigate, correct and boldly discharge as God's mouthpiece. By the voice of prophets battle has been won in the Old

Testament profile. By prophet's vocal leading an axe edge floated, disobeying the law of floatation which states that; heavy object sinks but by prophetic mandate, the reverse was the case .The Bible says "by a prophet the lord brought Israel out of Egypt, and by a prophet was he preserved." *If the mouth of your prophet can not preserve you, change him" or you're chained* when he's violating his prophetic ethics and grace.

In the same vein, prophetic voice of instruction should not be relegated. There was a case of a woman who when she was in immigration mess was guided prophetically not to show up on a particular occasion when she was summoned, she ignored the voice of Prophet and listened to the voice of friends and from there she was deported back to her native country not to mention of many that have despised Prophetic voices and traded it for the voice of professionals now, they are grounded at the end of the day.

Naanam was so lucky to heed the prophetic voice before he was cleansed of his leprosy. Otherwise, his hope of healing would have been dashed. Thank God for the wonderful maid he had. May I ask you, has the voice of your Doctor, Consultant, Bank, Lecturer or Lawyer replaced the voice of your prophet? When medical findings informs you that you can't survive it and your prophet says the opposite which one do you believe?

I was on campus years ago in Nigeria where a girl came with a condition of virginal discharge. During counselling, I told her to go to the toilet and check up herself the first time, she came with no result, the second time a felling of dryness and third time she came back completely whole. Similar to Naaman you can not afford to underestimate the efficacy of prophetic voice.

A woman came to me in Dublin three years ago for her son to be prayed for but God spoke to my heart that she has more pressing issue than her son's case then she voiced and told me of how she had become object of mockery because she only changed cars but could not own a property of her own like other colleagues in her profession so I prayed and mandated her to go and begin to look for the house of her choice. But she replied and said. "Sir, I don't have a healthy account and credit history to pursue this" nevertheless, she obeyed. At the time frame I gave her, she owned her own house. Tell me what God cannot do by the voice of his prophet.

Years back, a prophet in my life gave me a word that I will be a writer and gave certain instruction to which I obeyed, honoured and guarded diligently; it was witnessed by my wife. Systematically, as time went by, the voice of that day has become a reality today. Now, you are reading the mysteries of voice.

Listen, **obedience to the voice and counsel of God's prophet can make you to jump the queue, move you from the waiting list to priority list.** Now, get ready for your healing, new level, new contract and strong relationship. Be ready, to move from bitter to better relationship with God and men. If the voice of your doctor or consultant informs you that this sickness will kill you and your prophet say you will not die but live; which voice will you believe?

When we had our son, the doctor told my wife in my presence she'd live with some symptoms among which is a chronic headache and back pain and after the doctor finished with his message, I turned to my wife and said, you will never experience any of them. Three years now, that report has remained invalid. Whatever you believe determines your getting.

1 Samuel 1: 17-20 (NKJV) *Eli answered "Go in peace, and may the God of Israel grant you what you have asked of him." She said, "May your servant find favour in your eyes." Then she went her way and ate something, and her face was no longer downcast. Early the next morning they arose and worshiped before the LORD and then went back to their home at Ramah. Elkanah lay with Hannah his wife and the LORD remembered her. So in the course of time Hannah conceived and gave birth to a son. She named him Samuel, saying, "Because I asked the LORD for him."*

Shiloh was an annual traditional thanksgiving audit of blessing, where every family converged to register their appreciation to God. Hannah was there but could not worship. Upon her encounter with the prophetic voice of Eli, her annual sorrow was converted to everlasting joy and her time of sorrow came to an abrupt end because of her confidence in the voice of her prophet.

The following morning, her downcast face turned to broadcast joy and in due course, she became a mother of Samuel a renowned prophet of God. Wow! A prophet's voice released a prophet child. The voice of Eli was the answer to the bitterness of her life. Despite the state of his relationship with God at that moment of time God still honoured his voice.

What a pity today, powerful voices like this have been ignored and left many grounded in their journey of life and faith. It is a wise choice, to listen to your prophets and respect their voices because it downloads from God. And mark this, God has not given you the mandate to scrutinize and assassinate them character wise. Prophetic voice has the tendency to shorten your life's journey. Ignoring it can elongate it.

How about the false prophets? *Deuteronomy 18:20 (NIV)* *"But a **prophet** who presumes to speak in my name anything I*

*have not commanded him to say, or a **prophet** who speaks in the name of other gods, must be put to death".*
Ignore such voice. Attack it with all your strength. It is like a wicked rod and will not rest on you in the name of Jesus. Be deaf to such a voice, put it to death in your life and give it a silent burial.

Pray Along

- I deactivate and neutralise evil voice of prophet troubling my life, family and business in Jesus name.

Voice of Jezebel

1 Kings 19:1-3 (NKJV) *And Ahab told Jezebel all that Elijah had done also how he had executed all the prophets with the sword. Then Jezebel sent a messenger to Elijah, saying, "So let the gods do to me, and more also, if I do not make your life as the life of one of them by tomorrow about this time." And when he saw that, he arose and ran for his life, and went to Beersheba, which belongs to Judah, and left his servant there.*
Jezebel was the wife of Ahab a wicked king. What a misery, a wicked queen to a wicked king .An idol worshiper to the core with an inherited garment of paganism.

This type of voice leads people away from the worship of true God to the worship of idols. It motivates, promotes and encourages immoralities. It Decoys, lures, tricks, entices, distracts and detours people's heart from the path of righteousness, holiness, decency and faithfulness to spouse. It injects loss of will power, faith, discipline, integrity, uprightness, denial of faith (apostasy), believe and principle. She represents a voice of snare or distraction.

This evil voice can sour a sweet relationship between husband and wife, father, mother and their children, Pastor and members, employer and employee. It gives reasons why the husband must cheat on his wife and divorce until the family is wrecked. It encourages absence in church services and gives a time table of how you must fellowship with God and avoid the gathering of the saints. And why you must not pay tithe, harbour sins in the gathering of saints under the camouflage of civilization.

It catalyses lies, envy, backbiting among people etc.The list is endless. It can make someone who has promised you to disappoint. It can entice to sin when you have made up your mind not to. Don't read or study the Bible, sleep a little and as Proverbs said "A little sleep a little slumber all tends to poverty, don't pray, watch movies, have sex even when you know it is wrong.

This voice will sound so hard, so strong, that you loose your will power until you succumb. This is a voice of Jezebel it is all over today in the church, family and society at large.

But as you are reading this book, the supreme voice powered by the Holy Ghost will silence them in your life in Jesus name. The time of its control and rule over your life is over and such voices are silenced in the name of Jesus.

1 kings 19: 1, 10, 13, (NKJV)

And Ahab told Jezebel all that Elijah had done also how he had executed all the prophets with the sword. Then Jezebel sent a messenger to Elijah, saying, "So let the gods do to me, and more also, if I do not make your life as the life of one of them by tomorrow about this time." So it was, when Elijah heard it, that he wrapped his face in his mantle and went out and stood in the entrance of the cave. Suddenly a voice came to him, and said, "What are you doing here, Elijah?"

Consider Elijah the Prophet of God, an anointed man of God after a great feat and victory over the Prophets of Ball. This voice intimidated, frustrated and attacked him to the extent that he considered suicide as an option .The same yardstick she employs to attack any man that dared to challenge her evil control. If this can happen to a great prophet man of like passion like us, it can happen to us as well.

He became so frustrated that this woman's voice changed the course of his life from city to wilderness in the cave where he had no mission or assignment. Whichever cave you are in now get ready to come out.

Perhaps you have been raised like Elijah as a Pastor, teacher, or an Apostle who stands against immorality in your community and you have suffered a set back like Elijah you don't need to give up or quit, do not throw in the towel, the voice that commissioned you will preserve and protect you. I prophesy that every voice that has sent you a strange mission, changed your life's direction against God's will is condemned in Jesus name. The regime of a misleading voice in your life is over. Your mission will not come to an abrupt end.

The voice of Jezebel will not live long. It will not escape judgment. Something happened, this voice did not last for ever, Jezebel's voice was silenced by a supreme voice, her body was eaten up by dogs and her voice was never heard again. Every voice of Jezebel in your life, school, workplaces, church, family, controlling you, your parent, guardian husband, wife, boss, will not survive this month in Jesus name.

Listen you've got to voice back. What a pity, Elijah was able to silent prophets of Ball but not Jezebel; I know some voices are like that of a strong man but God who avenged and fought for him will fight for you too. Where your voice is not winning the unquestionable voice of God will defend you, your business and interests.

Voice of Goliath

1 Samuel 17; 1-52

This is another typical satanic voice and I refer to this as the voice of the terrorist. Biblically, it is the voice of a ring leader of the Philistine army. This voice sounds to destroy confidence, it invades and pitched tents in peoples heart of perception, challenge authorities, undermine self esteem, retard progress, pronounce untimely death, abort destiny and testimony particularly when you have a promise.

It unleashes physical and verbal assaults. Rehearse to your hearing the weight of past failures and harness why you must not believe otherwise. It enforces its opinions in contrast to your wish and beliefs. It tells you why you failed, and must fail again. It shows you the mountain and pretends to you there is no valley, pronounce restlessness, alters the state of tranquillity.

Always it calls for a battle with the intention to exile, introduce confusion and unusual standstill into families, churches, careers, faith, and pronounce a curse which

ultimately is set to defile the name of the Lord in your life.
*43." So the Philistine said to David, "Am I a dog that you come to
me with sticks?" And the Philistine cursed David by his gods."*
Many like Goliath did, had been cursed by the name of one
god or the other but was David quiet, crying or depressed?
No. 1 Samuel 17:3-4 says *"The Philistines stood on a mountain
on one side, and Israel stood on a mountain on the other side, with
a valley between them and a champion went out from the camp of
the Philistines, named Goliath, from Gath, whose height was six
cubits and a spa"*

Genealogically, Goliath was not a Philistine by race but
from the mighty races of giants whom Israel fought when
coming out of Egypt. Goliath's ancestors had been Israel's
enemies and Joshua annihilated them all, except the
inhabitants of Gath where Goliath hailed from. Why are
these details so important? Because if you leave your old
enemy, the evil voice, a leg to stand on, he'll rise to speak
again.

He was a youth (Na'ar in Hebrew) and in contemporary
English a boy or lad probably still in his teens too young to
be a man but note this, he acted like a man, voiced like a
man. This guy came on behalf of Philistines and held the
whole Israel at ransom for 40 days. I don't know the
duration of your ordeal with this uncircumcised giant the

time to come out of it is now. The voices that attack you in dream must be buried in Jesus name.

He has earthly armour, stature (Height) and backing of gods but no celestial garment.

Goliath has five parts to his armour;
- Helmet of brass
- Coat of mail
- 2 greaves for legs
- Breastplate
- Spearhead

These I consider his assets but conversely, they were David's liabilities. Now, see what a different perspective can make. When they all could see a giant by revelation, David could see a mortal man a teenager for that matter, hired to defy and defile the God of Israel.

I don't know what the assets of your Goliath are, the origin, maybe from water (marine powers), from the rock, principalities, witchcraft, sorcerers or ancestral stubborn spirits. Don't be intimidated by the weight of their names and gravity of their description. A sling of stone from your voice will defeat them. Some may trust in Horses and chariots but we will trust in the name of the Lord. The name of the lord is a strong tower the righteous run in and they are saved.

That voice that has been challenging your health was not silenced because you can only hear the voice of a giant and his boasting about past records of Cancer, Arthritis, High blood pressure, Diabetics, poverty, addiction, divorce, anger and depression, unsettled family or broken home, untimely death, late marriage, joblessness, cycles of failure, limited speed in life affairs, lack of harvest after laborious planting, failures in ministry. This voice had bombarded your heart with uncountable voice mails that keep playing one after the other that you have almost believed, that it is your turn and you cannot escape it for any reason eh! I want to tell you such voice is a voice of Goliath and must be silenced.

I do not know how long or how far. The purpose of this book is to find you and deliver you from such a voice and you are declared free, now in the name of Jesus.

There is nothing special you need to do than to check mate the voice. Do this in good time; don't leave it too long for hours, days, week, months or years like King Saul. You have been ordained the king of your family, business; ministry and career. Speak back in good time and delete all the Goliaths voice messages in your heart. **The heart is the centre processing unit for all voices that enter through** your ears; it is the last bus stop of every message, not the head or your mind.

I remember my early days in ministry, lying on my bed in hostel on campus after a lecture. Three women appeared to me in my room (Federal University of Technology) where I was the Vice President of the fellowship and sounded this terrific warning to me in anger under a horrible laughter saying; "carry on with deliverance and keep loosening all our preys".

They said unanimously, "are you not going to get married? Keep doing it, we are watching you" and they suddenly disappeared but the voice did not, leaving me perplexed for some moments. Without wasting much time I came to understand the message, got up from my bed, stretched forth my hand and said in the name of Jesus perish.

To my surprise that evening I went ahead to pass a night with my aunt a nurse by profession. On my arrival she requested me to pray for a neighbour whose case had defied medical attention. That patient was advised in the hospital to go and seek spiritual attention because he had been spiritually attacked.

This was a Polytechnic undergraduate who could not walk with his two legs which he described to me as heavy as two bags of cement (wickedness is real). After God revealed to me the secret of the Goliath behind this young man's illness, by the power of the Holy Ghost, I gave a voice of assurance to him that he will walk again. I employed the weaponry of vocal power and by the grace of God Samuel is now a graduate. Referring to the beginning of this testimony, voice, like that of Goliath came to attack my heart knowing I was going to set free one of their preys that day but I attacked the voice in good time and was able to liberate that young man.

Maybe as a minister of the gospel, voices have warned you not to embark on that task for God and that if you do it, your family is at risk, and your office is at stake. Just leave the demons alone, let them do their work. You face your own business yet you have this voice and mandate to set the captives free.

My advice; do not listen to such voice. Develop the heart of David who did not subscribe to people's criticism and intimidation. He knew the importance of taking action with God to fight for him; he realized there was no reason to wait. People may try to scourge and discourage you with negative comments, voices, or mockery, but continue to do what you know is right.

You must dare to challenge, silence and disgrace those voices that have been sounding from generation to generation and nobody to silence it, telling you its feats over your ancestors.1 Samuel17:45-47 (NKJV)

Then David said to the Philistine, "You come to me with a sword, with a spear, and with a javelin. But I come to you in the name of the LORD of hosts, the God of the armies of Israel, whom you have defied. This day the LORD will deliver you into my hand, and I will strike you and take your head from you. And this day I will give the carcasses of the camp of the Philistines to the birds of the air and the wild beasts of the earth, that all the earth may know that there is a God in Israel. Then all this assembly shall know that the LORD does not save with sword and spear; for the battle is the Lord's, and He will give you into our hands."

Goliath overturned the peace of the entire country suddenly and enthroned panic and fear in a country with such a might and the first king in Israel. I suppose it targets the career of Saul as the first king in Israel but the devil is a liar. Every voice targeted or aimed at your office as a prophet of God, as the man of the family or instrument of change in your generation, the Lord will arrest in Jesus name.

At last, Goliath was silenced by little David. **It is not a question of how big you are but who is in you.** At last your Goliath will be silenced. For forty days, twice a day, Goliath's voice sabotaged the business empire of Israel in order to ruin their economy. It imprisoned their freedom of speech and lifestyle, as some lifestyles have been suddenly altered just because of the voice of a Goliath.

Some career has folded up , businesses closed down, projects stopped or suspended indefinitely because of a Goliath, sleeplessness persists, properties lost, home lost, the entire holiness of God in the land defiled by an uncircumcised voice, until an unquestionable voice sounds through the mouth of David a shepherd. May such unquestionable voice disgrace the Goliath of your life in Jesus name.

Goliath just like Jezebel was not left without judgment. Every evil voice has an expiry date and time, they cannot and will never exceed their labelled time if you take the right action, as David did (1 Samuel 17:48-49). David listened to the voice that instructed him to use irrelevant but effective weapon that the war marshals' would have condemned and followed the voice of instruction that played from his heart's voice mail and he recorded a gallant victory over their then prime enemy Goliath. The Bible recorded, with a sling and stone vs. 51.

Vocal instruction is vital for fatal victory. *If you ever have a Goliath, look at the David inside of you.* The Philistines so much believed in Goliath, that they doubted he could not die so cheaply but when his head was cut off and displayed after his death, they became sure of his death. They turned back and ran. David took custody of the Philistine's weapon in his own tent having acted promptly and swiftly.

Do not be in a hurry to tidy up well, a lesson from David. Max Lucado writes, "we retreat behind a desk or crawl into a nightclub, or a bed of forbidden love. For a moment we felt safe, insulated, anesthetized, but then the work runs out, the liquor wears off, the lover leaves, and we hear Goliath again...."Rush your Goliath with God's saturated soul." David selected five stones from the brook. Here is one of the five stones you can use to defeat the enemy:

The stones of past success, recalling and rehearsing his earlier victories, David declared,' *God who delivered me from the lion and bear, will deliver me from this Philistine'* (1 Samuel17: 37) *'write your defeats in sand but carve your victories in stone* by voicing to the Goliath the records of God's faithfulness and the marvellous works he has done'. Has he ever failed you? No, and he won't now. You can't stare at your giant forever.

Rehearsing your hurts won't heal them and cataloguing your problems won't solve them. I prophesy your Goliath will die this year. All the Philistines of your life will run and come back no more. God has given you the power it is in you; it is in your voice. Use it!

Note this, until you defeat your Goliath, you may not assume the throne. The worst the Devil can do is to silent you but in Jesus name where your voice has been buried and the power of your voice has been ignored, this time around, the world will hear your voice as you are plugged and connected to the supreme voice through Jesus by the Holy Spirit.

When unquestionable voice sounds, every power bows. "He has given him a name that is above every name and at the mention of his name, every knee shall bow. Understand this you have been given that same name. Use it, and it will work for you.

Voice of Sanballat and Tobiah

This often sounds or originates from human agents who are secret enemies that manifest in time of great adventures. They are anti- restoration, anti-rebuild and evil rabbi who emphasise disadvantage over advantages. They slow down or rather bring a progressive movement to a halt, lovers of wreckages and shambles, patriots of demolition, devastation, inspiration killers, and they are agencies that recruit mediocre; particularly in form of close friends, passers by, and demon inspired people. They plant the seed of discouragement in order to steal distinction.

In the church they are satanic accountants who count the cost and kill the vision. They keep tradition at the expense of revelation. In establishments they oppose changes and fail to learn new methods that can enhance productivity and efficiency. They are old and blurred in vision to perceive optimistically. They are not ready to go and they pollute the heart of the willing with their toxic voice. They initiate destructive competition in favour of monopoly.

In friendship, their voice contaminates and provokes envy. Their voices declare a promise that will never be delivered in order to establish stagnancy. This type of voice inspires people to make vows in the church and refrain to redeem their vows in order to make names and assassinate the vision.

They intrude into affairs of peaceful families with their voice in order to produce another corrupt one like their own kind. They wash noble ideas down with their voice and promote the ignoble. Their vocal cords are readily available for satanic use. They make profit in shameful ventures as opposed to promising visions.

Nehemiah 2; 10, 19, 4; 1-7, 6; 1-4 13-28   *Then I went to the governors in the region beyond the River, and gave them the king's letters. Now the king had sent captains of the army and horsemen with me. When Sanballat the Horonite and Tobiah the Ammonite official heard of it, they were deeply disturbed that a man had come to seek the well-being of the children of Israel. But when Sanballat the Horonite, Tobiah the Ammonite official, and Geshem the Arab heard of it, they laughed at us and despised us, and said, "What is this thing that you are doing? Will you rebel against the king?"*

Vs7 Now it happened, when Sanballat, Tobiah, the Arabs, the Ammonites, and the Ashdodites heard that the walls of Jerusalem were being restored and the gaps were beginning to be closed, that they became very angry.

When Nehemiah made a move in his heart to reconstruct the wall of Jerusalem which was wrecked by Babylonians invasion and restore the worship of the living God, they were not happy because he wanted to erase the Babylonians' footprints.

Nehemiah, a man of prayer, having accumulated enough grace and courage in the place of prayer obtained the favour king and got a letter of recommendation or order for safe conducts with entourage to facilitate his God given vision. Without him knowing, Sanballat and Tobiah showed up. They were naturalized enemies who were not indigenous Jews.

Despite their vocal contaminations and pollution, Nehemiah did not give up his task because he has an asset.

The voice of power he obtained in the place of prayer furnished with passion and determination he spoke back to his two major enemies.

You have woken up, from dreams many times with strange voices that challenged your progress and God given vision, marriage and business. What should be your next point of action? You don't have to lie down crying all day celebrating those voices of discouragement that flux in to cripple your God given vision for your life.

For you to take your business, ministry, career, education, family to the next level, ignore such voice and delete their messages from your mind. Get up again to attain that great feat because time is not on your side. I don't know who you have decided to marry and you have obtained approval from God yet you're intimidated hear this story my father told me.

When he heard the voice from God about whom he was going to marry, his best friend was like a Sanballat; he asked him these questions; "how dare you? What is you academic qualification? What is your CV, a poor Pastor to a Teacher?" And when he had finished all his vocal discharge, in his story, he did something that's note worthy, he ignored him and his voice and ran with the voice he originally heard. When he was going on his first visit, he went with friends who had a vocal agreement with him and abandoned the options of Bank manager, lawyers, lecturers she could have married. Till today, they are both happily married and in Christ.

Maybe this is your case. You have been deformed by your friend's voice that you are not qualified to marry that man or that woman because of your past, perhaps the broken wall of your life they know about and Babylonians impacts and foot prints in your life had given them the impression that you deserve nothing better based on their knowledge about you.

My advice is, get up now. Go for it and if you can adopt Nehemiah's principle and embrace his ethics it will be yours and you will laugh last.

The twelve gates were rebuilt. I saw all these gates when I went to Jerusalem. The reconstruction was made possible by the vocal strength of a man. I don't care how many of your vision has been truncated, sabotaged. You can start from there now. *Anywhere is a starting point.* Your starting point does not determine your end point. Many started poor and ended rich. Many started rich and ended poor.

We all have assets and liabilities. Convert your liabilities like poor background, lack of finance, poor education, dry prayer life, temperament, envy, laziness, procrastination, race, colour, to assets by trade-in principle. Use your assets to gain more assets. Cause the dot of your life, family, business, marriage to tend to the positive direction. Add value to your life and move forward. Ignore negative voices and turn your negatives to positive. Initiate the project and complete all the twelve walls of your life that nations may come and worship your God.

Those who said God cannot use you again are not the supreme voices. You can be relevant again. Rahab the prostitute made a record. Peter the extrovert became the rock. Jabez the son of sorrow became honourable. Saul the persecutor turned to Paul a preacher. College drop out turned to a millionaire and employer of graduates and sinners of yesterday turned to saints.

You have the assets; salvation, Holy Spirit and the voice. As a result, take a giant leap. This is your time. *Don't sit down idle anymore issue a red card to your adversaries.*

Nehemiah overcame ridicules by prayer and hard work. Opposition by determination and holy anger, threat of war by prayer and preparedness and Jesus overcame by prayer and fasting. **Behind every great vision is a great opposition** You have the voice to overcome every strange voice. Speak back and act fast. Trust in God because it is your turn to overcome. *If you listen to the voice of opposition, it will make you loose your position.*

You can say amen to this prayer;
Your destructive critics will end up in crisis and I declare by prophetic voice, every thing that stands still in your life to gain uninterrupted speed and what has fallen apart will begin to fall in place in Jesus name.

Voice of commission

Isaiah, "whom shall I send"---. There is a cry in heaven in constant search for those who will be his mouth piece.
*Then the LORD said to Moses, "See, I have made you like God to Pharaoh, and your brother Aaron will be your **prophet**.*
Exodus 7:1 (NKJV).

From the scripture above, it can be inferred that voice gives you identity and responsibility that is specific for a particular task. God is not after the experts or somebody with reputable character. When it comes to his choice for assignment, his business empire is compounded and busy that he recruits people regardless of their background, colour or races to prepare for his own use.

Whenever He makes His choice nobody can question Him. But there is something that characterizes His appointment. He always backs them up with his voice which stands to be the support system any calling, mission or commission should be founded on. The government employs this practice on appointment of ministers.

If God orders for it, He will pay for it. There is no need to be afraid. If He says go; that is exactly what He meant. This knowledge will keep you going when the going is rough and tough and He is faithful.

I don't know what you have been commissioned to do by God. You heard the voice and you are sure of who spoke to you. As a result, don't give up. Count on his voice. It never fails because in this voice is honour and glory. It is a noble voice to be trusted and relied upon.

The reason why you doubt is because you doubt the voice. It is ever active and alive. It never failed on Jesus; it will not fail on you. It doesn't matter if things have fallen apart, they will fall back in place.

Judges 6; 14, 16 & 24 *Then the LORD turned to him and said, "Go in this might of yours, and you shall save Israel from the hand of the Midianites. Have I not sent you?" And the LORD said to him, "Surely I will be with you, and you shall defeat the Midianites as one man." Then the LORD said to him, "Peace be with you; do not fear, you shall not die."*

The voice of the Lord came to Gideon, when his life was in shambles and his future was dark. Being under the attack of the Medianites was not easy joke but he was energized. He shook off the beast, pursued his mission, carried out his assignment fearlessly and was delivered from the imminent death penalty that could have ended such a task.

Note this, It doesn't' matter, if the world's book of record has not documented such a task, achievement, business or whatever. As far as God is leading, go ahead and execute it.

I was asked about eight years ago by an ex- president of my fellowship when I was an undergraduate of which voice I heard from God that encouraged me to stay glued to healing and deliverance? I then took a deep breath and replied the voice of encounter I had during 56 days fasting and prayer which clearly said to me "Do you know anything you say we do and anything you decree we establish?" This voice mentioned to me the name of my best friend and my hostel room number. Though, I was fidgeted and highly flabbergasted, but I strongly believe it.

This same voice of encounter is the fountain of my progress till today and will remain forever. It keeps playing in my heart like a rhythm, anytime the going gets tough.

The Lord called Moses not his brother or sister. He commissioned Abraham not Lot. If he commissioned you, He is more than able to provide, protect, sponsor and defend you. To protect his integrity of commission, God dealt ruthlessly with Miriam, Moses' sister with leprosy when she was messing with the grace of assignment upon Moses. He is in position to do the same for you but, be rightly positioned. Don't fight the battle yourself, wait for your defender. *If God hires you, nobody can fire you.*

It is worthwhile, to enjoy the power of vocal backing and support from the supreme voice at the place of assignment and mission.

Not limited to this, Apostle Paul was not left out, in Acts 18: 9-10 (NKJV) *9 Now the Lord spoke to Paul in the night by a vision, "Do not be afraid, but speak, and do not keep silent; 10 for I am with you, and no one will attack you to hurt you; for I have many people in this city." 11 And he continued there a year and six months, teaching the word of God among them.*

What a powerful voice of promise, may be you are planning to call it quit now or about to throw in the towel; listen, the voice that converted Saul was the same that insured his assignment and the Bible says he continued there a year and six months unhurt. I pray you will abide in your God given assignment.

Another instance is in Acts 22vs 11 -12. *But the following night the Lord stood by him and said, "Be of good cheer, Paul; for as you have testified for Me in Jerusalem, so you must also bear witness at Rome." And when it was day, some of the Jews banded together and bound themselves under an oath, saying that they would neither eat nor drink till they had killed Paul.*

The voice of commission stood by Paul and delivered him from the plot of his determined Roman enemy who went into covenant, embarked on black, dry fasting in order to kill and end his ministry but their enterprise failed; I see God doing the same thing for you. Listen, ***you're not fit to die until you have delivered victory to humanity.*** In Jesus name you will abide in your God giving business, mission and assignment.

And lastly, *Matthew 3; 16-17 (NKJV)*
16 When He had been baptized, Jesus came up immediately from the water; and behold, the heavens were opened to Him, and He saw the Spirit of God descending like a dove and alighting upon Him. And suddenly a voice came from heaven, saying, "This is My beloved Son, in whom I am well pleased."
*While he was still speaking, behold, a bright cloud overshadowed them; and suddenly a voice came out of the cloud, saying, "This is My **beloved Son**, in whom I am well pleased. Hear Him!"*
Matthew 17:5 9 (NKJV)
*for He received from God the Father honour and glory when such a voice came to Him from the Excellent Glory: "This is My **beloved Son**, in whom I am well pleased."*
2 Peter 1:17 (NKJV)

The greatest mistake anybody can make is to get on a ministry, task or business enterprise without a voice of commission. It will just be like a house with no foundation that can collapse at anytime.

Going without this voice displays lack of support system and it can predict unceremonious seizure. If Jesus can't dare it, why would you? Before you step out, wait for a voice to guide, announce and instruct you, the voice of John the Baptist was vital for Jesus ministry therefore, in business, investments and life career wait for the voice.

Voice of vengeance

The account of Cain and Abel is a classic illustration in the Bible of a voice that cries for vengeance, it turns the voice of God to voice of indignation. "The voice of honest indignation is the voice of God." William Blake (1757 - 1827). Genesis 4:6, 8-12 *So the LORD said to Cain, "Why are you angry? And why has your countenance fallen? Now Cain talked with Abel his brother and it came to pass, when they were in the field, that Cain rose up against Abel his brother and killed him Then the LORD said to Cain, "Where is Abel your brother?" He said, "I do not know. Am I my brother's keeper?" And He said, "What have you done? The voice of your brother's blood cries out to me from the ground. So now you are cursed from the earth, which has opened its mouth to receive your brother's blood from your hand. When you till the ground, it shall no longer yield its strength to you. A fugitive and a vagabond you shall be on the earth."*

Believe it or not there are many problems that are direct consequences of the voice of vengeance. A crying voice, architected by aborted pregnancy; blood of the unborn crying for vengeance, unjustified frame up that has led to incarceration, imprisonment, loss of jobs, positions and opportunities that are somehow not repeatable in lifetime. Unknown covenant of ancestors from parents knowingly or unknowingly particularly occultism, past promiscuous life of illicit and unscriptural sexual acts, slavery, manslaughter, assassination both of character and life.

Many cannot confidently say amen to such prayers as "May you harvest what you have sown'. I know, that, there is a law of sowing and reaping, law of fullness of time, law of seed time and harvest and law of gravity 'what goes up must come down; this is just the reality.

Nevertheless, there is a provision under the New Testament, *unto Jesus the mediator of a new covenant, and to the sprinkled* **blood** *that speaks a better word than the* **blood** *of Abel. Hebrews12: 24 (NKJV).*

A similar instance in New Testament was the voices of scribes and Pharisees who are conscious of the law but ignorant of grace and so sued for vengeance on the woman that was caught in the very act of adultery. **John 8:7-11**
"He who is without sin among you, let him throw a stone at her first." And again He stooped down and wrote on the ground.

Then those who heard it, being convicted by their conscience, went out one by one, beginning with the oldest even to the last. And Jesus was left alone, and the woman standing in the midst. When Jesus had raised Himself up and saw no one but the woman, He said to her, "Woman, where are those accusers of yours? Has no one condemned you?" she said, "No one, Lord." And Jesus said to her, "Neither do I condemn you; go and sin no more."

Grace silenced the voice of her adversaries. The voice that acquitted and vindicated this woman of questionable character is still actively at work today to do the same for you. It doesn't matter anymore the location and direction of this voice, outside or within the church, when and how those voices that have condemned and asking for vengeance on you, they will be silenced in your family, ministry, and business in the name of Jesus. So, this woman escaped the penalty for her ill doing.

It does not matter to God, how bad what you are harvesting now is or what you are supposed to reap lawfully. Each time you are being hunted and hurt by your dirty past, promiscuous life style and evil investments, there is a grace of exit. I have dealt with cases of people asking me "could this be from my past or a result of such and such covenant?" But all I answer them is there is a New Covenant.

In that He says, *"A new covenant,"* He has made the first obsolete. *Now what is becoming obsolete and growing old is ready to vanish away. Hebrews 8:13 (NKJV).*

All you need do is to subscribe and key in, into the freedom package of the New Testament voice made available by the blood of Jesus. It takes blood to speak against blood" any voice of vengeance wailing on your business, family and marriage is silenced for ever in the name of Jesus and you are set free unquestionably.

PRAY ALONG

- I receive the grace to believe and honour the voice of my prophets.
- Oh lord, send the voice of instruction, direction and information that will change my weekly income to daily income, my monthly income to weekly income.
- Every financial friction, struggling and annoyance, receive divine lubrication by the forces of voice.
- Evil voices that manipulate and amputate my destiny die in the name of Jesus.
- Ancestral evil voice that operate in my generation I command you die in Jesus name.

- Holy and only father, restore all I've lost by disobedient to the voice of your prophets.
- Henceforth, I paralyze every voice of Jezebel, voice of vengeance operating in my life.
- I command voice of Goliath in my family, ministry and business to die in the name of Jesus.
- Lord, disgrace every voice of Sanmallat and Tobia threatening my progress.
- I silent in the name of Jesus voices of Sanbalath and Tobia challenging my progress
- Voice of vengeance the blood of Jesus speak against you
- Grace silent the voice of my adversaries, voice of oppositions and oppressors.
- Voice of vengeance your rule is terminated in the name of Jesus.

Chapter

3

The Supreme Voice

Unquestionable Voice

Dear reader, this is the most prophetic aspect of this book, I candidly advice you to read these pages with full expectation that will produce a dramatic turn around in your life record. In this segment, something beyond description will happen in your life because the voice I am about to discuss here is all you need. The unquestionable and the supreme voice could be interchangeably used in this part.

Since I caught the revelation of the unquestionable voice, things have assumed a new dimension in my life and ministry. I as well know, it can change your entire world, move you from waiting list to priority list hence you will jump the queue.

My first preaching on this concept was characterized with two minutes miracles seasoned with sequential healings of sinusitis, broken leg and sore throat from birth for thirteen years. What an amazing meeting. You can expect and receive your own miracle now.

Let me introduce to you the unquestionable voice. It is immutable, ethically pure, above reproach and by antecedent principle, unquestionable. The voice of the unquestionable God has been from the beginning of the world and it is older than age. It is relational in nature, gentle in correction, mingled with unlimited promises of comfort. It can bring something out of nothing, does not lie. This voice can deliver whatever He promises.

The voice is unlike that of a politician, or one president whose word can change. Politicians make promises they can't fulfil because they are limited in power and have no power over death.

If God says to you "do not be afraid", you can go and sleep. That is the unquestionable voice. I remember his voice spoke to me shortly after my final exam in the university as I was driving home just about two minutes from my college premises contemplating about what my results would be and it said to me "if my voice has ever said to you do not be afraid, you better believe than doubt. I tell you I could not keep this voice I immediately conveyed this message to every one I came in contact with. His voice can make you an ambassador of his goodness. When the result was out, it was 2nd class honours.

I respect the omniscience and omnipresent power of this supreme voice. In the bush, in the waters, in the fish's belly, in the valley, on the mountain, anywhere in the world, this voice transmits wirelessly. It can reach anywhere and anybody at anytime. It bypasses every human and spiritual defence to reach its target. It is not restricted by cells, tissues or organs. It can fix, replace, repair, renew and redress. It is unfailing, infallible, dependable and reliable. It can't be limited by technology or any mechanical device. In fact; it can give voice to a stone. Living, non living, animate and inanimate responds to the stimuli of his voice.

The supreme voice of God cannot be validated neither can the depth of its wisdom be fathomed. It is invisible and yet produces visible results. This voice can dethrone and enthrone. It hardened the heart of Pharaoh till he was destroyed yet unquestionable. He can promote unquestionably without any human reference. He can initiate unceremonious departure of age long invader of your harvest.

He is unlimited in influence and access. He spoke through the mouth of a Donkey. It is not subject to distance or location. This supreme voice created life and protected it. By and through this voice, a virgin became the mother the saviour of the whole universe, boycotting and violating human and natural law of reproduction. This voice is unstoppably powerful, faster than the speed of light, it can reach anywhere at anytime.

The voice can compel, constrain, correct, control and convert. It can select, seclude, separate and sanctify. It can do, and undo without any challenge. It can answer all manner of questions and silence any debate yet unquestionable. Its' answer to sickness is healing; to poverty is prosperity, failure, success, rejection acceptance.

The accuracy of supreme voice

Mark 11:2, 4. *And He said to them, "Go into the village opposite you; and as soon as you have entered it you will find a colt tied, on which no one has sat. Loose it and bring it. So they went their way, and found the colt tied by the door outside on the street, and they loosed it*

The supreme voice accurately and timely located this useful, but tied down, healthy but forgotten, overlooked and restricted colt. May be you are tied like the colt, useless and abandoned; this voice will locate, relocate and reinstate you. Your skills and talents that are esoteric will come to limelight. He will mobilise human and spiritual forces to facilitate this in the name of Jesus.

Acts 9:1-4 (NKJV) *Then Saul, still breathing threats and murder against the disciples of the Lord, went to the high priest and asked letters from him to the synagogues of Damascus, so that if he found any who were of the Way, whether men or women, he might bring them bound to Jerusalem. as he journeyed he came near Damascus, and suddenly a light shone around him from heaven. Then he fell to the ground, and heard a voice saying to him, "Saul, Saul, why are you persecuting Me?"*

This voice is a force. It can arrest and cannot be resisted. It caught up with Saul on his way to Damascus, arrested him, changed his plan and commissioned him. It doesn't matter the credentials of your pursuer and persecutor, how long or how far, there is a voice unquestionable. It will arrest, convert and recourse them to promote your cause to the path of fulfilment.

The reasons and motive of Saul on his way to Damascus was changed, to promote the gospel of Christ he was contesting. *Your pursuers of destiny are simply and sincerely wrong.* You will move and achieve in the name of Jesus. Who is that king, boss or power that is oppressing you, denying you of your promotion and infringing your rights.

Believe this, from this moment, the unquestionable voice will dethrone such without contest. Every chaser of your life and destiny would be detoured by his unquestionable voice

Noble Man at the Gate of Destiny

In Esther 6; 1-10 is another super act of the unquestionable voice. *That night the king could not sleep. So one was commanded to bring the book of the records of the chronicles; and they were read before the king. And it was found written that Mordecai had told of Bigthana and Teresh, two of the king's eunuchs, the doorkeepers who had sought to lay hands on King Ahasuerus. Then the king said, "What honour or dignity has been bestowed on Mordecai for this?"And the king's servants who attended him said, "Nothing has been done for him." So the king said, "Who is in the court?" Now Haman had just entered the outer court of the king's palace to suggest that the king hang Mordecai on the gallows that he had prepared for him. The king's servants said to him, "Haman is there, standing in the court." And the king said, "Let him come in." So Haman came in, and the king asked him, "What shall be done for the man whom the king delights to honour?" Now Haman thought in his heart, "Whom would the king delight to honour more than me?" And Haman answered the king, "For the man whom the king delights to honour, let a royal robe be brought which the king has worn, and a horse on which the king has ridden, which has a royal crest placed on its head. Then let this robe and horse be delivered to the hand of one of the king's most noble princes that he may array the man whom the king delights to honour. Then parade him on horseback through the city square, and proclaim before him: 'Thus shall it be done to the man whom the king delights to honour!'" Then the king said to Haman, "Hurry, take the robe and the horse, as you have suggested, and do so for Mordecai the Jew who sits within the king's gate! Leave nothing undone of all that you have spoken." So Haman took the robe and the horse, arrayed Mordecai and led him on horseback through the city square, and proclaimed before him, "Thus shall it be done to the man whom the king delights to honour!"*

Mordecia could be referred to contemporarily by his passion as a Human Right Activist. He cried so much at the gate that his voice couldn't be heard in the palace. On this memorable day of supreme intervention, unquestionable voice interrupted and intercepted the king's sleep to catch his attention. In the morning, the book of remembrance was opened and the record of his loyalty that had been buried was exhumed.

Mordecia, a victim of omission was remembered. He experienced a dramatic change of position. He moved from the gate into the palace, his garment was changed. He moved to the presidential suite and began to enjoy continental treatment. He became an honourable man translated from a horrible to a noble position. His determined enemy was humiliated. His intention to annihilate mordicai and his race was aborted.

When the unquestionable voice collides with your destiny it has the mandate to exhume, moisturizes and revitalize your destiny. "The very you at the gate, that was unknown before is another you in Palace". I doesn't matter how long your promotion had been delayed, denied, or your good works had been ignored or overlooked. The supreme voice is set to arrest the comfort of your benevolence and something compensational is about to happen. Your pitiable condition will be transformed to dignified position.

All you have been doing is your best in the family, at work, church and community but all they could see are your faults and flaws .You are wondering what you have done wrong and hardly believe if the situation would ever change. Relax; the unquestionable voice will speak on your behalf.

I know there are some people you cannot approach by virtue of your status. Your spouse is there but you cannot reach her, there is a big gap between you and your potential husband. Is there somebody who had refused to pardon you, favour you or is tantalizing you with your entitlements and rewards? It is time the unquestionable voice will sound to such and all your benefits will be relinquished.

Here is an awesome testimony. During counselling with a brother who was an undergraduate Chemistry student in a renowned Nigerian University, it became obvious to me that a voice ruling the family system stems from his fathers senior sister. His father was a successful cocoa farmer and at any harvest season, this woman will call his brother and remind him of a court case he must revive and without resistance this man would lavish all the money that harvest season on the case.

As the case was, cocoa business in Africa is seasonal and whatever cannot be accomplished at a particular harvest season is deferred. At another season she would summon his brother and remind him he needed to marry another wife and he would comply without hesitation. This continued till the man died, all because of a voice in control of his family with fatal consequences on the children.

After this, at age ninety she continued with this brother's son who was a class representative. This old woman's voice will mandate him to stop during examination and when the examination was about to close she would release him and whatever he wrote would not be enough for him to pass. He began to experience decline in his academic performance because he could not finish on time anymore in class test or examination. He began to build up carry over courses until the day he was delivered from this voice.

Before her ruling was ruled out, she confessed all the evil she had perpetrated in that family including when this young man was driving and she ordered him to release the break of a van when it was unsafe to do so. The car crashed, but he escaped death.

Tragically, this old woman died after he was delivered and he is now a graduate and doing fine in the Lord. With this testimony, you should now be sure that the evil voice controlling your life adversely and sponsoring your adversities will die in Jesus name.

The Egyptians haven subjected the Israelites to severe servitude, denied them of their right to go and serve God but at their exodus from the land of slavery, they disgorged all their gold and silver to them. The powerful men who caged your help will respond to the supreme voice now and they will be chasing you about with goods and gold. Unquestionable voice will visit the tumour regions in your body and destroy cancerous cells, go to your blood cells and heal every form of diseases. Remember this is a voice of power you can check your healing now.

This voice had fixed a broken leg, healed sore throat that has lasted for thirteen years, corrected eye defects (Myopia). Now, it is your turn and in the name of Jesus, receive your desired healing now. This voice will architect that sudden change you need now, in Jesus name.

I pray for you that:

Every voice that has buried your good works and rewards, the unquestionable voice will exhume and will disentangle every cobweb around your destiny in the name of Jesus.

PRAY ALONG

- Supreme voice, speak to all that matter about my promotion, contract and my career.
- The powerful men that detain and cage my testimony; it becomes fire release it now in Jesus name.
- You deadly disease; Cancer, tumour, hear the voice God die in the name of Jesus.
- Unquestionable voice, withdraw the comfort of my stubborn helper to deliver the desired help to me.
- Unquestionable voice, swallow every voice that sponsor fear and defeat in my family, business and ministry.
- Every difficult situation that resist changes in my business receive supreme visitation.
- Unquestionable voice put a stop to every arrow of delay fired at my progress and promotion.
- Unquestionable voice, establish a divine connection that will move my business to the top.

- Every evil plot to destroy my testimony, fail in the name of Jesus.
- I command in Jesus name stability to my breakthrough.

Chapter

4

Pathways to Validate Voice

Validation from the science point of view, consist of the process or steps involved in ensuring, that an equipment do as what it purports to do. The result is synonymous to the condition of the equipment.

Having recognized that voice is a powerful device, it therefore becomes vitally important to know what to do in order to ensure it works properly and enjoy its maximum use and impact in the entire coverage of our life.

This becomes so essential in operating a powered voice; with no resistance that the devil trembles at, sickness bow for, dreadful to principalities and powers, rulers of darkness in high places, command angelic response and capture heaven's attention.

Integrity link

Integrity is a great attribute that has no limit in boundary. It is not the gift of the spirit, but what we all need to develop. This is because it has a strong link with good intentions and moral dispositions. It requires you to constantly probe your intention and scrutinize your motives. It enables you can avoid ignoble acts as they can pollute and diminish your vocal strength.

Your voice must be able to withstand and survive integrity panel. It starts from as little things like your cheque book, which is your voice. It says, "Pay this amount to this person". Bounced cheques are a demonstration of lack of integrity.

In the same way, vow is a function of voice. An unpaid vows and pledges to God and individuals is a lack of integrity. Promise, they say, is a debt. Do not promise what you cannot do neither do this out of duress or pressure. It will eventually fracture your fidelity and integrity. For your voice to command respect, get honoured by men and heavens, pay attention to this.

Much business voice had been killed because of lack of integrity. They advertise on insincerity and falsehood claming it is just a business gimmick. No wonder the brand

and business name is buried silently by unsatisfied customer. Can your customers patronize you? Do you have satisfied customers any more?

There was a case I know of many years back of this person who habitually come late to work but signed in early to show he was in on time. On this faithful day, he became a victim of his voice when an incident happened at work and all the staff on duty at that time was suspended by the management.

In reality, he was not supposed to be connected with the case. But record proved him. His voice put him in trouble. What a great lesson.

Repair your integrity pole and validate your voice. Don't abort the plan of God for your life.

Integrity cannot be underestimated in executing divine assignment as seen in Acts 19:11-20 (NKJV).

Now God worked unusual miracles by the hands of Paul, so that even handkerchiefs or aprons were brought from his body to the sick, and the diseases left them and the evil spirits went out of them. Then some of the itinerant Jewish exorcists took it upon themselves to call the name of the Lord Jesus over those who had evil spirits, saying, "We exorcise you by the Jesus whom Paul preaches." Also there were seven sons of Sceva, a Jewish chief priest, who did so. And the evil spirit answered and said, "Jesus I know, and Paul I know; but who are you?" Then the man in whom the evil spirit was leaped on them, overpowered them, and prevailed against them, so that they fled out of that house naked and wounded. This became known both to all Jews and Greeks dwelling in Ephesus; and fear fell on them all, and the name of the Lord Jesus was magnified. And many who had believed came confessing and telling their deeds.

Also, many of those who had practiced magic brought their books together and burned them in the sight of all. And they counted up the value of them, and it totalled fifty thousand pieces of silver. So the word of the Lord grew mightily and prevailed.

If you have no integrity, demons, sickness even men will ignore your voice. Evil spirit can identify the voice of integrity. They said to the seven sons of Sceva,"Paul we know, Jesus we know but who are you? They ended their day with disgrace. That should not be your portion. Do all you can to be a man of integrity

To be integrity gang star could be devastating. Living as parasites on people's integrity could be unhelpful while reliance on other people's integrity is tantamount to laziness and lack of self esteem. The raw material to build your integrity is right there with you it is a personal responsibility you cannot afford to shirk.

During a counselling session while writing this book, I was exorcising a spirit and when I command it to leave; I asked "do you know who's talking to you"? The spirit could relate with my identity and said", I am a warrior "then I replied "having known that, you know my mandate and you have no ground to remain here now, therefore, go" and the spirit left immediately. I even commanded the spirit to take along a stone planted in that body causing serious ailment and send it back to the sender. Wahoo! What power integrity can exert in the spirit realm.

Peter and John at the beautiful gate exhibited integrity. They had no money to offer to the lame man, God honoured their voice and healed the lame man. This miracle gave them the platform via integrity to declare the gospel of Christ with an audacious voice that grabbed the attention of all Jews.

Many Christians today have the right currency, even gold that can answer that need, and they still want to pray for what cash could answer. Can we be real and stop wasting the power of prayer?

Do not substitute prayer for what integrity can answer. Learn to be integrity conscious. It counts in validating your voice. *Integrity is the structural framework of identity*. Do not limit the strengths of the voice God gave you. It is a weapon on earth and a means to penetrate the celestial and spiritual realms.

Purity link

We must be aware of the fact that we are constantly surrounded with things that are unclean with the tendency to pollute our heart and mind. In schools, offices and in the atmosphere around us nowhere is free of these germs. The only way to survive is the constant reading of the word of God, application of the blood of Jesus and the help of the Holy Spirit to conduct a heart surgery and give us new heart.

Clean water cannot flow through unclean channel. The word of God is like water it is clean and can cleanse. John 15:3-4 *You are already clean because of the word which I have spoken to you. Abide in Me, and I in you. As the branch cannot bear fruit of itself, unless it abides in the vine, neither can you, unless you abide in Me. (NKJV).* The most efficient detergent that guarantees constant spiritual sanity of heart is the word of God (voice). Its efficacy and efficiency have gone beyond ages of which I am a witness. Hear God's comment in Genesis 6:4 *The LORD saw how great **man**'s wickedness on the earth had become, and that every inclination of the thoughts of his **heart** was only evil all the time.* Also Mark 7:21- 23 laid emphasis on this; *For from within, out of the heart of men, proceed evil thoughts, adulteries, fornications, murders, thefts, covetousness, wickedness, deceit, lewdness, an evil eye, blasphemy,* *pride, foolishness. All these evil things come from within and defile a man."* **'You cannot say it better than your heart.** It is the main voice. Thus, to retain all time healthy heart condition, all time cleansing is inevitable.

As mentioned earlier, the heart is the central processing unit of humans and you are a product of your heart condition. Your voice can not be better than your heart and mark this, **the quality and quantity of your voice is a function of your heart.** Matthew 12: 34 Brood *of vipers! How can you, being evil, speak good things? For out of the abundance of the heart the mouth speaks.*

From the scriptural accounts above, it becomes clear, that purity link delivers quality and quantity or volume to your voice. Spiritual heart surgery is therefore required. If you can validate you voice you'll become valid and ready for God's good use.

The heart revolves around four things; what you see, read, hear and watch. Daily and constant bath in the word of God keeps you clean and with the Help of the Holy Spirit such that you become a clean channel for God's flow.

Power link

Ephesians 1: 19-20... *and what is the exceeding greatness of His power toward us who believe, according to the working of His mighty power which He worked in Christ when He raised Him from the dead and seated Him at His right hand in the heavenly places,*

The voice of a king or queen is strongly connected with the power associated with the royal office. The voice a Prime minister is directly proportional to the power associated to his office. Hence, **the strength of a voice is the product of the power working within.** As a Christian, you are connected to an unfailing power which is the power of the Holy Ghost. Hallelujah.

It does not matter who you are, your size, age, weakness or strength, once this power is in you, you are no more ordinary. Your voice carries weight, respect and authority that can't be quantified by any physical parameters cutting into the spiritual and physical realms.

By their fruit you shall know them, it is of no good to be plugged and not connected. The power at work determines the quality and quantity, durability, dependability, viability and availability of the fruit of your voice. Some things respond to certain authority. Elijah on the mountain said if I be a man of God, let fire come down. *2 kings 1: 9-12 (NKJV).*

Then the king sent to him a captain of fifty with his fifty men. So he went up to him; and there he was, sitting on the top of a hill. And he spoke to him: "Man of God, the king has said, 'come down!'

So Elijah answered and said to the captain of fifty "If I am a man of God, then let fire come down from heaven and consume you and your fifty men." And fire came down from heaven and consumed him and his fifty. Then he sent to him another captain of fifty with his fifty men. And he answered and said to him: "Man of God thus has the king said, 'Come down quickly!' So Elijah answered and said to them, "If I am a man of God, let fire come down from heaven and consume you and your fifty men." And the fire of God came down from heaven and consumed him and his fifty.

Here is a typical power link exemplified by Elijah the prophet. His voice commanded fire. Without delay, one hundred and fifty two soldiers with two captains inclusive were roasted in fire. His voice became a weapon. The third captain bowed to his voice and he and his men were spared hear what he said *vs.14. Look, fire has come down from heaven and burned up the first two captains of fifties with their fifties. But let my life now be precious in your sight."*

His territory became unapproachable. It is not a fairy tale but a reality. It all depends on the level, source and extent of connection to the supernatural. The effects and impact of your voice is dependent on the power at work in you. When I was young in faith, I prayed hours to heal a headache. Not now sicknesses don't wait for me to finish before they take their leave unceremoniously.

When Jesus was to be arrested in the Garden, he simply asked, whom are ye seeking? *John 18:6Now when He said to them, "I am He," they drew back and fell to the ground.* This portion of the scripture really thrilled me. It is important to realize from this scripture that we are not born victims. The power in his voice was so irresistible. It electrocuted his arresters. You must not settle for the less.

Your voice must begin to swallow that of your foes and challenge whatever dares you. The only way is to get connected with the power of the Holy Spirit (remain online) so that you don't live below covenant promises. The power that generates your voice is paramount to the effects, consequent result and impact it exerts.

There are some health conditions, financial conditions and problems that generally defy human and medical attention. Such may have a backbone of spiritual, inherited strongmen that will only yield to a voice of power.

A nurse came to me with a health condition of high blood Pressure and diabetic. As I sensed it in the spirit the case was inherited I rebuked the spirit behind it. Immediately, all the symptoms vanished. She went to her Doctor the following week and came back with good news that her blood pressure is normal. May be you are in the same condition I rebuke the sickness from its root in Jesus name.

Prayer link

We are quickly found of defining prayer as a two way communication between God and Man and that is from the Christian perspective, but most often we fail to cogitate on the fact that the word communication; is more of a heart issue than mouth. Thus, I describe prayer, as coming into union with God's mind.

God showed Jesus everything He was thinking and said to His son, "Go and manifest that for me". We need to know that **there is nothing more intimate than your thoughts.** Voices are extension of our thoughts, but we are our thoughts.

When our prayer life transcends mouth regions to the level of relationship with God, just like Jesus, he begins to show us what he was thinking in our hearts he expect us to go and manifest it for him

To validate your voice, is to be in a position that heaven can constantly, without inhibition, download God's intentions into your heart. "Thy will be done on earth as it is in heaven".

God expects us to speak like him and get results and none of his word has ever gone unfulfilled. It therefore becomes so important to get close to him, and develop a voice that is vulnerable enough to convey his wishes all time. Voice is trained and empowered in a place of constant and consistent fellowship with God in prayer.

Let us consider Jesus' model of prayer;

When we spend time with God in the morning, or anytime, He begins to show and say to your mind what's supposed to be said in fact your hearing senses is tuned. Many of us say we believe this principle, but we really don't. We put off praying because we think it is a waste of time, or at least less important than other activities. We also think the length of time we pray isn't important but there is need to learn from Jesus disciplined life of prayer. He first talks to God every morning before he talks to any man. *If you can hear from God, men will be forced to listen to your voice.*

Sickness, circumstances and situations will respond to your commands. One experience I have always enjoyed in the place of prayer is the confidence of my vocal strength. There is more you will get in His presence than you can accomplish in the presence of other people. You spend all day talking foolishness with others who aren't contributing anything to your future. Let's shun empty voice and get into prayer.

We spend time to discuss trivial issues, politics and gangs for two or three hours. In the end, nothing is solved, nothing has changed and you are depressed. Such time should be converted to prayer. We often discover that when we spend time in prayer, God begins to use us to change circumstances and situation.

There are eight watches the Hebrew observe each day. These watches, will compound your tenacity in prayer. At the Wailing Wall all, the Hebrews observe these watches. I witnessed this when I was in Jerusalem. At every given hour, there are people there praying.

Acts 3:1 (NKJV) Now Peter and John went up together to the temple at the hour of prayer, the ninth hour". We must learn how to watch in prayer. There are some things that one watch cannot address it takes two to three watches to breakthrough them. When you finish, a feeling of strong relief and ability clouds you up with the confidence that your voice is empowered.

Mark 1:35 35 (NKJV) Now in the morning, having risen a long while before daylight, He went out and departed to a solitary place; and there He prayed.

Jesus, after despatching the disciples and the crowd, went somewhere to pray .Having accumulated much presence; He was ready again to manifest the thoughts of God through his voice. God does not generally speak verbally He speaks directly to our hearts and prayer makes us so confident to voice out what God is saying into our hearts and what you say will be heard.

Altar of prayer

You need to set up an altar of prayer and do not allow any man to abuse your prayer life. People will always place demands on your prayer time, by phone calls, etc. It all aims at depleting your efficiency. When you have a burden that no man can off load, manage to the place of prayer it will suddenly disappear. Devil will always block you but ignore his devices. Do not leave your phone on while praying. Do not expect any caller or any important call. It will impair your concentration and pollute your consecration on the altar. Let people respect your prayer life.

Jesus ignored the crowd. I don't know who or what your crowd is? Before you can cross to the other side of greatness do the same. During your break time at work; pray, if the day is too busy, use an option of night vigil. *If you don't have a custom of prayer you can't have the custom of victory.* You must be able to cut four to five hours of your sleep staying all night with God in prayer at least once a week or fortnightly. I remember the day God told me that my sleepless nights with him is the raw material of my prosperity. Stop late movies and start night prayers.

Speaking in tongue is also a way to validate your voice. When speaking in tongue, you are emboldened and can speak without fear as someone under influence, not of hard drugs but of the spirit. After the experience in Acts 2: 14 *But Peter, standing up with the eleven, raised his voice and said to them, "Men of Judea and all who dwell in Jerusalem, let this be known to you, and heed my words.*

There are occasions you need to speak, respond to or preach. You are either shy or coward like Peter, but after sessions of serious tongues he became drunk in the Holy Ghost and so high. He raised his voice and preached boldly a seemingly endless sermon hallelujah.

There are many decrees you will not be confident to issue over situations and circumstances unless you're bold and out of your mind into his mind. God is looking for people like this. There are some voices that employ the service of angels, cherubim & seraphim and some command the response of the hosts of heaven.

Recently in London I was ministering somewhere .While I was speaking in tongues, a Wizard spirit spoke and said to me "why are you are binding me"? But the mystery is I was speaking the language that only the host of heaven can decode and they carried out the assignment. You cannot underestimate the strength and result that characterize speaking in tongue.

No wonder the devil is doing all he could to discourage and hinder people of God from enjoying this gift. Praying in the spirit emboldens you and you can speak with confidence Hence your voice becomes an authority. Pray in the spirit in the car while driving. I enjoy this. It does not in any way impair your concentration.

Talking gymnasium

There is something I have consistently noticed in migration history, it amazes me how people can easily change and pick up assent. A migrant to America picks up American assent, to Britain, British accent, to Africa and so on and I wonder what factors could have contributed to this. Then I came to realise that practise, interest and duration of stay are major catalysts.

I met an octogenarian Irish priest who was a missionary to Africa and spent nearly most of his life there. He speaks most of the native language and his English flavoured with African assent.

Talking sessions could be dated back to creation. It was institutionalised by God with his first graduate being Adam in the Garden of Eden University. . Genesis 2: 19b-20 (NKJV) and *brought them to Adam to see what he would call them. And whatever Adam called each living creature that was its name. So Adam gave names to all cattle, to the birds of the air, and to every beast of the field. But for Adam there was not found a helper comparable to him.*

All creatures answered the name given to the by Adam till today I believe they are the generic names that are later translated to scientific names. Talking session is a spiritual gymnasium whereby you practise faith speeches to ventilate polluted atmosphere that surrounds your life, family, ministry business or career. Speak to things that were not as if they were until they begin to materialise.

Whatever you call them, they will answer. Now, what do you call it, cancer, poverty, impossibility or possibility, death or life? In the long run, the blame is shifted to the devil oh! If the Devil could reply he would attribute it to your inefficient use of voice.

You can register in this school of thought now. If it appears a problem call it progress. If it appears poverty, call it prosperity, as sickness; sound health, as death call it life. David exclaimed and said; "I shall not die but live to declare the works of the Lord "(paraphrased). Talk it to actualization. Rehearse and emphasis on why you should live.

A similar account in; Ezekiel 37:1, 2, 4. *The hand of the LORD was upon me, and he brought me out by the Spirit of the LORD and set me in the middle of a valley; it was full of* **bones**. *He led me back and forth among them, and I saw a great many* **bones** *on the floor of the valley,* **bones** *that were very* **dry**. *Then he said to me, "Prophesy to these* **bones** *and say to them, 'Dry bones, hear the word of the LORD!*

The spirit of the Lord (Holy Spirit) took Ezekiel into the valley of dry bones to build his vocal muscles. It was dry bones scenario. Here his voice pattern changed as he was under the tutelage of the spirit. What an amazing experience. Before you could become an approved voice of God this experience in your life is inevitable.

Step wisely. As he was speaking, his voice rearranged and assembled the architectural outfit of the dry bones until they became a living soul.

Mark this; your voice cannot be trained in the valley of living bones. The face of hard and harsh situation is the practice field to develop the strength of your voice, declaring the words of faith and holy incantations. When in the wilderness the voice of the devil came to Jesus "jump down," "turn stone to bread" and Jesus replied "thou shall not tempt the Lord your God. He continued his advances and Jesus persistently replied until he desisted.

Keep talking to the situation until it is changed, recognize your authority and he who is with you. Begin to prophesy until lifeless business gains life, toxic relationship becomes exotic. In these talking sessions, your voice changes from pessimism to optimism.

Here, the promises of God become Rhema. Don't be a talkative, instead articulate, and appropriate the countless promises of God. It is the voice of God. "Faith is kept alive in us, and gathers strength, more from practice than from speculations" Joseph Addison.

Get this clear; the secret of successful public performance is a sincere private practise. If you can practise in private you can be approved for the public.

Before God will release you to be his public voice he must validate your private practise to avoid shame and disdain of his glory.

Say to this mountain move. The reason why many mountains remain is with your consent and it couldn't even realize somebody is talking. Why? It's due to the fact that they cannot relate with your voice. Matthew 12:33

*"**Make a tree good** and its fruit will be **good**, or **make a tree** bad and its fruit will be bad, for a **tree** is recognized by its fruit.*

Speak until a desired fruit is seen. Set back is nothing but a set up in disguise for good. Speak things that were not to come into existence. Change your route plans from gossiping to faith gymnastic.

PRAY ALONG

- Holy and only father, pardon all my injustice and abuse of integrity.
- Holy and only father confer on me the grace to trade and transact with integrity.
- Holy Father, I pray today give me a voice that demons cannot challenge.
- I challenge every assault launched against my prayer life.
- Now, Holy Ghost fire, revive my prayer life and restore dignity to my voice.
- Every adamant situation resisting change melt as I pray now (mention them) for God is a consuming fire.
- My voice is empowered today in the name of Jesus

- Every great door shut by lack of integrity be opened by grace in the name of Jesus
- I command sanity to the polluted atmosphere of my life in Jesus name.

Chapter

Treatment of voices

Ignore or listen

*If anyone does not listen to my words that the **prophet** speaks in my name, I myself will call him to account.*
            -Deuteronomy 18:19 (NIV)

I wonder how people are encumbered with counselling stuffs. Many have developed a resistance because they failed to listen, or as much as they do, they ignored at the same pace. James 1; 22-23

But be doers of the word, and not hearers only, deceiving yourselves. For if anyone is a hearer of the word and not a doer, he is like a man observing his natural face in a mirror; for he observes himself, goes away, and immediately forgets what kind of man he was.

An unbalanced equation will remain a mathematical problem. In the linear equation of listening plus hearing, doing is the balance. The paramount thing is to be the doer. Being a consistent listener does not make a perfect doer.

Do is the key not ignore. Ignorance has no place in the law. In fact, it is a crime that is punishable. Change your method, change your approach from obsolete to contemporary for a better result .If you are not ready to change you will be chained. Put an end to late arrival syndrome. Do it now and stop telling stories and lamenting that 'I have heard about it before' the question is what you have done about it?

I heard of a communication business in 2005, and I signed up to be a consultant yielding to a voice of direction. I embarked on it and became so successful that I and my wife were sent on an exotic all inclusive holiday to a seven star hotel in Turkey in 2006 where celebrities patronized. It was an experience of pleasure that can't be eroded from my memory.

The degree of your enjoyment is synonymous with response to the right voice. If any evil voice comes to you do not listen. Give such voice a silent burial. We bother too much about many things that are not necessary due to lack of knowledge. The voice you listen to will eventually control you. Set yourself free today from such negative voices and enjoy freedom and peace. It is aimed at stealing your peace to leave you in pieces once again but never give a chance.

Furthermore, do not resist the efficacy of the voice of God in his words. There is blessing for being the doer; go and be one. Stop attacking and stop resisting. Do it immediately. Go and invest, do it now, knowing that, some opportunity present themselves only once in a lifetime, while some can be repeated. Can you answer which forms is the potential of that chance you want to ignore? **Opportunity must meet preparation for a click**. The voice could be for a life time turn around for prosperity, fame or healing.

Finally, a family friend who is a physiotherapist by profession and the husband a medical Doctor shared this with me many years ago while talking about the significance of voice. She used to have this terrible migraine every time she went to the salon. This condition defied medical attention until she listened to a voice not from any man of God or as a result of a crusade or miracle service. That voice said she should stop using a particular hair cream. To her surprise, the migraine vanished the very day she listened and yielded to this voice.

How long have you been ignoring the voice that tells you to stop doing certain things which could have facilitated your miracles, healing also bring blessing, and greatness to you in life, but you resistively ignore and opted for the other choice. The ball is in your court, it would be a wise decision to yield to the voice of God and ignore any other voice. It is contrary living to embrace the voice of the devil at any stage.

Lots' wife ignored the voice of God and she became a pillar of salt all because she decided to disregard. Now that you are still living, do not trade the voice of the Holy Spirit for the voice of friends, economy, doctor or any other voices. Stop that business now and reinvest in another so as to avoid a catastrophic loss. Do not doubt. It is just the right time to make a change. Not all that glitters are gold'.

Faith

Faith is different from belief. It is characterized by works or resultant action to what you believe. It is hopping for what you have heard, anticipating with corresponding positive actions.

A voice of power may come to you today and may stay a thousand years unperformed because it is not supported by the necessary action. This does not suggest that the word is weak in the mouth of the spokesperson. The Lord cannot compromise his stand about faith. "Faith without work is dead   "

As the body without the spirit is **dead***, so* **faith** *without deeds is* **dead***. James 2:26 (NKJV)*

The work is not God's part, it is your part. King David said; (paraphrased) 'your word oh lord is settled in heaven'. If God says anything, it remains valid, settled, stable and unbroken regardless of time. Until you activate it with your faith action.

The workability of a voice in your life is tantamount to your responsive faith actions' the fact that it was said, does not guarantee it will happen to you if you care not to respond quickly. The fact that it is not happening now will not make God a liar. By two immutable thing in which God cannot lie. Whatever is not done in faith is sin. So, it is the question of your sin not God.

God sent me to a couple and I told them," that God said He wants to favour you, unaware of what their experience was three years later, she came back and said from the first day I gave that word, their entire life experienced a dramatic turnaround and rearrangement. That was the outcome of her faith. That's what will happen to you too. Wahoo, faith in Gods' words will rearrange your life profile, flavour you and increase the volume of your achievement.

Peter Boehler said to John Wesely; "live by faith until you have faith". I visited a family three years ago. As I was about to leave, a voice said to me 'ask if it was their decision to have only one child".

Unanimously, they said no; I simply requested them keep a date that day and I left. Few weeks later, the woman's absence in services became conspicuous and I asked why. She replied "you said it sir". To the Glory of God I was the god father of their baby girl. It should be clear enough to you now that treatment of voice with faith produces results. If you desire a child, get it in the name of Jesus.

Learn to fear the voice of God in reference. Don't doubt it. The opposite of faith is fear and my acronym for FEAR is False Evidence Appearing Real. Fear can only be eroded from your heart by digging in the well of God's word to develop your faith.

I recommend that you doubt your doubt not God. Any voice of despair, like that of Goliath, (voice of terrorist), Samballat and Tobia, death sentence telling you that you can't make it again, and other negatives you should ignore. Put your absolute faith in the voice of God, his prophets and positive voices of people. Your faith can make anything happen. Invest your faith in the best asset and it will definitely yield dividend.

Zachariah became dumb following the message from angel Gabriel. Even though he occupied a priesthood office he could not relate with the voice in faith and he became dumb and was unable to speak until the day of fulfilment of that voice. In other words, he became disabled and the voice remained active.

Doubt, is a strong weapon of spiritual and sometimes physical disability. It is so vital to have faith in the given words and the spoken words of God. Many have declared many things that failed to materialize and yet blame God. Check yourself, internal auditing. Was it spoken out of faith? His words are yea and amen.

Sometimes ago, a woman came to me about her son who was the source of sorrow to her family. She expected serious prayer but all she needed was a word. I advised her to go home, revitalize her love for this child and say good things about him first thing every morning and before he is twelve years old, he will be totally restored. She went back and acted on this instruction in faith. Today, the boy is a better lad now.

The best Treatment to the words of God is with faith, speak with faith and you cannot be put to shame for God honours faith.

Obedience

1samuel 15: 22; So Samuel said: "Has the LORD as great delight in burnt offerings and sacrifices, as in obeying the voice of the

LORD? Behold, to obey is better than sacrifice,   And to heed than the fat of rams.

Obedience brings great delight to God more than anything else. Sacrifice can not replace or substitutes for the pleasure it brings to God. This suggests that the opposite, disobedience brings displeasure to God. Partial obedience is no obedience at all. It is poisonous, God frowns at it. *Deuteronomy 8:20 (NKJV). As the nations which the LORD destroys before you, so you shall perish, because you would not be obedient to the **voice** of the LORD your **God**.*

"No principle is more noble, as there is none more holy, than that of true obedience" said Henry Giles. It is a true evidence of reference to God's holiness. It is an important fruit of the spirit and the nature of God. As a fruit, it must belong to a vine. It means that it is produced by a power. A power working in a plant determines it fruits.

There are different qualities of fruits; fresh fruits. Your obedience must be fresh not stale. Varieties of fruits suggest your obedient must be unconditional, abundant without limit and abiding, it must be consistent. These are the qualities of obedience.

Mary said, to the servants, "Do whatever he tells you." John 2:5 and this act of obedience created the land mark of miraculous conversion of water to wine. I pray with you, as you begin to obey more and more, unusual, uncommon and seemingly impossible events of supply will bombard your life.

Obedience will process the water of your life to wine. Obey that voice that is asking you to give knowing that, the water signifies the source not your labour while the wine is the resource.

In Israel, marriage is not possible without wine. At the point of Shame and disgrace, obedience to the voice of Mary and to Jesus voice turned their shame to glory and resulted in a miraculous provision. Obedience can supply the wine you need in your marriage, ministry, business and progress in life. Do not set up your obedience on conditions. In the case of marriage which took place at Cana in Galilee, the servant's obedience extended from Mary to Jesus. *Network of obedience breeds chains of testimony and possibilities.*

Jesus said to peter, Luke 5:4 (NKJV) *When he had finished speaking, he said to Simon, "Put out into deep water, and let down the nets for a catch."* after a busy night of labour without results, a net breaking miracle attended his way. Obedience can make you hit a contract of lifetime prosperity. It can move your business, church and account from 3 to10 digits, it can flavour stinking relationship and reinstate broken homes.

Instead of giving up, why not obey. It may demand you to obey the voice of God or to do a simple thing to get out of a mess. The situation will remain messy if you fail to obey. Obedience delivers prosperity and posterity.

At times, you may need to PRAY through, but the disobedient heart says it does not require prayer. My wife after a classic send off party in her office flanked with beautiful pictures and gifts got a call from her boss that she would have to stay for some reasons. She got home sad and I was also disturbed with this news more so when she's got a date to commence her new job.

The Lord asked me this question and I forwarded it to her that' "did you Forget or Left something behind that you need to pick up in that Egypt?" She calmly replied "No"; that voice clicked in her and she nodded I told her to immediately book a hotel and escape to a "mountain" to do it herself. She obeyed. Two days after she came back she got a letter, apologetically revoking that message. Why? She obeyed and prayed. Do the right thing and get the right result.

Your case may be to PAY through. Go and sow a seed to a ministry or somebody's life. Remember Abraham Pay through. He hospitalised the angel. He was ready to pay his only son;

Genesis 22:12-14 (NKJV) And He said, "Do not lay your hand on the lad, or do anything to him; for now I know that you fear God, since you have not withheld your son, your only son, from Me." Then Abraham lifted his eyes and looked, and there behind him was a ram caught in a thicket by its horns. So Abraham went and took the ram, and offered it up for a burnt offering instead of his son. And Abraham called the name of the place, The-LORD-Will-Provide; as it is said to this day, "In the Mount of the LORD it shall be provided."

Abraham obeyed God's voice to sacrifice his only son. What a robust and absolute obedience. But God made a provision and his rewards transcends generations. I tell you, vows and gifts have opened many doors in my life. Change your slogan that says money is not everything. Have a holy mouth.

Finally, you may need to PRAISE through. Paul and Silas in the prison praised. Neither money nor prayer was relevant at that given time. They applied the right principle and the result was so instantaneous that the prison door swing open. I don't know what your prison is. If praise is the key that must open it, every other means will fail. I am so convinced that your obedience appetite is so high now.

Isaiah 1:19 (NKJV); If you are willing and obedient, you shall eat the good of the land. Deficiency of good things is coming to an end now. It is time to obey and to eat good fruits in life. Learn to obey and put a stop to struggling in your life. Due to disobedience to the voice of God and his prophets, many have lost substantially in businesses to fraudsters and in other gainful ventures, some have lost healing, spouse, etc but making a choice to tread the path of obedience now, the same way you lost, you will get all back and recover all by the pathway of obedience.

Regardless of your personality or position, if you negotiate your obedience, you will struggle in many ways, in healing, miracles and financial rewards. Though, God is the same yesterday, today and forever that is in the personality of Trinity; not in acts or word. He has divers' ways of operation.

Therefore, learn to obey his voice of instruction and you can experience stress free results. Wrong choice of co-workers in the ministry can bring about thorn in the flesh. Better obey. The Apostles said after the day of Pentecost, it is better to obey God rather than men.

I have experienced both sides of these treatments; obedience and disobedience and now can make my decision and constantly ask for the grace to obey. *1 Samuel 15:22."Has the LORD as great delight in burnt offerings and sacrifices, As in obeying the voice of the LORD? Behold, to obey is better than sacrifice, And to heed than the fat of rams.*

<u>PRAY ALONG</u>

- Every bitter harvest due to negligence, disobedient and rejection of God's voice and his prophets because of my repentance become well, and best.
- All I've lost be restored and as I continue to obey, let unusual testimony follow in the name of Jesus.
- In the name of Jesus I break into pieces the power and strong hold of disobedience in my life.
- I command abundance to replace the shortages in my life as I begin to obey.
- As I begin to obey and honour the voice of God and his prophets, let every detained blessings be released in Jesus name.
- Every evil pillars constructed by my disobedience fall in the name of Jesus.
- I open every shut door with the key of obedience and break every iron gates against my greatness this year.
- I receive plentiful grace to obey all the days of my life.

Chapter

You Can Create Your Own Future

But be doers of the word and not hearers only, deceiving yourselves. James 1: 22(NKJV)

You may not know that, denials of access to mysteries makes life miserable.

In this book, we have demystified voice in a robust dimension. Its potency as a weapon has been established. The mystery of creation is in the word "Let there be", a powerful voice that put the entire world in place. This voice suspended the earth without pillar, separated day from night and gave breath to all the living creatures including plants.

The knowledge of the fact that you are not a subject in this world; but an object will greatly regulate your mind. Coupled with the generously revealed truths about the properties of voice, types of voices, how to validate your voice, the unquestionable voice and treatment of voice will transport you back into the entire scope of God's agenda for your life.

2Chronicles 20:20. So they rose early in the morning and went out into the Wilderness of Tekoa; and as they went out, Jehoshaphat stood and said, "Hear me, O Judah and you inhabitants of Jerusalem: Believe in the LORD your God and you shall be established; believe His prophets, and you shall prosper."

God through the mouth of Jehoshaphat told the Israelites (paraphrased), "your wish is my command" then whose fault. Their voice determined their destiny. Many unknowingly have said they will die at a given age and it thus happened. Often times we commit crime with our voice and have suffered many things to this effect. A wise and cautious use of voice is therefore so important in order to preserve your life and wealth.

Voice can create a footprint for satanic operation such as slandering and backbiting men of God, fake promises and partial faithfulness like Ananias and Sapphira his wife. In *Acts 5:4-5 (NKJV) While it remained, was it not your own? And after it was sold, was it not in your own control? Why have you conceived this thing in your heart? You have not lied to men but to God."Then Ananias, hearing these words, fell down and breathed his last. So great fear came upon all those who heard these things.*

The weapon against this couple was their voice. They promised what they will not fulfil. This breach, granted death an access into their lives. They perished in a slow motion; have you ever taught of it?

The other fellow in Kings through careless use of voice activated death sentence. When the prophet declared there would be surplus he said in a loud voice it cannot be possible. The prophet of God endorsed his voice and at last, he was trampled by the crowd. He did not witness the bonanza according to his voice.

Psalm 1:3 (NKJV)

He shall be like a tree Planted by the rivers of water, that brings forth its fruit in its season, whose leaf also shall not wither; and whatever he does shall prosper.

Here the scripture figuratively refer to the righteous as tree. You cannot be one without knowing the proper use of voice. Attitude determines altitude no wonder the future of the righteous is so promising and bright because they have the power to appropriate their voice. Thus, it is very clear that the type of fruits your life produces is the product of your voice.

Matthew 12:33

Make a tree good and its fruit will be good, or make a tree bad and its fruit will be bad, for a tree is recognized by its fruit.

In other words, "voice good to your life and the proof will be good". You can create a good lifestyle, business, career, family, children, husband, wife and good church members.

The onus is on you not God. To decisively and consistently apply all you have read will change your entire world. It will strongly exert permanent changes into your family system, business, ministry and spiritual life.

Finally, you are the right person to shape your life. You can cerate your own future. You have been wield to do so. You are an operator by design not a spectator. Take the right step and begin to enjoy new fruits, fresh fruits, varieties of fruits, abundant of fruits and abiding fruits.

If this book has blessed your life, please share your encounter with the author.

Write to:
Omoniyi A.Akinnuwa
Divine Voice Impact
Unit 4, Dartmouth industrial Centre,
Kylemore Road, Dublin 10, Republic of Ireland

Call:
3531623-6838, 353851119696, Fax: +35314430795

Website:
www.divinevoiceimpact.com

E-mail:
abraham@divinevoiceimpact.com